Enfield Libraries

Branch:	R				
1/16					
14/11/19					

this item please call the renewals
0333 370 4700 or renew online at
yourlondonlibrary.net/web/enfield

ENFIELD Council

ANF
158.12

By

Brittany Samons

ENFIELD LIBRARIES

9120000054904

Table of Contents

Introduction 5

Chapter 1. How Meditation Reduces Stress and Improves Well-Being 7

Chapter 2. The Science Behind Meditation 12

Chapter 3. How to Start and What You Need 14

Chapter 4. Meditation Techniques 18

Conclusion 29

Thank You Page 31

Meditation For Beginners: Meditation Techniques to Relieve Stress, Calm Yourself and Your Mind, Achieve Inner Peace, Happiness and Stay Positive

By Brittany Samons

© Copyright 2015 Brittany Samons

Reproduction or translation of any part of this work beyond that permitted by section 107 or 108 of the 1976 United States Copyright Act without permission of the copyright owner is unlawful. Requests for permission or further information should be addressed to the author.

This publication is designed to provide accurate and authoritative information in regard to the subject matter covered. This work is sold with the understanding that the publisher is not engaged in rendering legal, accounting, or other professional services. If legal advice or other expert assistance is required, the services of a competent professional person should be sought.

First Published, 2015

Printed in the United States of America

London Borough of Enfield	
91200000549045	
Askews & Holts	Jan-2016
ANF 158.12	£3.56
1/16 ®	

Introduction

The mind controls our body and that is why it is most important to keep the mind and the body healthy and positive. The mind interprets what we see, what we hear, what we feel, taste, and even what we smell into thoughts. Naturally, thoughts are wild. Without our control, they easily come and go. Meditation, however, trains our mind to control our thoughts.

Our thoughts need to control, do you know why? The answer is simple. In the external world, there are many events and people that negatively impact us. That makes us think and feel negatively. When we keep pondering over those negative thoughts continuously, it negatively impacts our health, both mental and physical. Often, it is without our wish that these negative thoughts keep circling in your mind.

The mind is powerful and can be used to achieve the greatest good for ourselves and others, but it can also destroy our inner peace and health. Therefore, meditation, which includes many techniques to calm the mind and control thoughts, should be included in our daily life to keep negativity out of our lives even when we keep encountering it in our everyday life.

Chapter 1. How Meditation Reduces Stress and Improves Well-Being

Most of us can't avoid the stressors in our life. There might be difficult people at your office, you worry about the behavior of your teenager children, or you might have financial difficulties. These are some of the unavoidable circumstances that do not allow you to remain stress-free. Remember that there will be no time when there are no difficulties in your life. However, you can be stress-free despite of your circumstances by practicing meditation.

The most important characteristic of meditation is that it removes the negative impact difficult people and circumstances have on you. It trains your mind to think what you want it to think and absorb only what you want it to absorb. That is great power.

When you begin to practice meditation, you find that you are more aligned with your being, your soul, yourself. You begin to feel more comfortable with yourself. Irrespective of which method you use for meditating, you will experience great calmness. This is your natural state of being. The more you will stay in it, the more you will experience great calm and unrestricted joy. You will have to experience it yourself because what you will experience is hard to put into words. You will begin to enjoy the benefits of meditation from day one and they will continue to grow as you keep practicing.

Some of the benefits of meditation that you will see in your life are:

- Greater control over emotions

- Relaxed mind and body

- Improved concentration

- Reduced stress

- Significant reduction in negative thoughts

- Reduced intensity and frequency of depression

- Feeling of well-being and positivity

- Better memory

- More energy

Meditation also heals the body. You will find that your body is getting cured of lifestyle diseases such as high or low blood pressure, anxiety, heart problems, nervousness, stress, body aches, etc. It also helps in healing people of addictions and obsessions.

As negative energy and thoughts sap our energy, positivity and calmness increase it. Even if you are not suffering from any major illness or health problem, you will feel more energetic, calm, and relaxed.

Remove Stress Coming from Bad People and Situations

Imagine if you could just remove the bad people or situations that trouble you. You wish to, but you know that it is impossible. With meditation, that is exactly what you can do without physically removing bad people and circumstances. You can do that by stopping the bad thoughts that they germinate in your mind and take control of your mind by the hurtful actions of people or because of stressful situations.

All you need to do is to meditate every day, even if it is only for 10 minutes in a day. You are now given the chance to control over what you think. Even if you won't be able to control all thoughts, you will not be thinking negative thoughts again and again. When you begin meditating, you will instantly feel more healthy and happy, and will automatically begin to spend time every day practicing it.

Heal Yourself of Depression

It is the negative thoughts that accumulate and make us feel depressive. Sometimes, especially in women, depression and mood swings can be because of hormones. Depression originates in our subconscious state, and, therefore, we consciously cannot help ourselves get rid of it. The only way we can remove depression is to affect our subconscious mind and root it out from there.

When you meditate, your subconscious mind gets cleansed of negative thoughts. With your conscious mind, you remove sense stimulations of sight, sound, touch, taste and smell. You sit with your eyes closed, do not move, and remove all distracting sounds from around you. In this state, you are helping your conscious mind to disengage from sense objects. When it does that, it begins to realize what lies beyond the conscious mind. In this state of meditation, you feel eternal calmness and peace. Your mind heals itself of all bad and hurtful feelings, thoughts and actions. A few minutes in this state are enough to completely relax and de-stress you. Even after you have begun your daily life, you continue to feel its calming effect for hours.

Chapter 2. The Science Behind Meditation

How does meditation work? What does it do to our mind? Is there any scientific explanation to how the mind responds to meditation? These are some of the primary questions that anyone beginning in practicing meditation has.

It is a known fact that meditation impacts the neurotransmitters in the brain and also our DNA. Scientists have found that those who practice meditation for years have high levels of the hormone called DHEA. This hormone is known to slow ageing and fight diseases. Many of the benefits of meditation are not yet scientifically proven, but they are felt and realized by those who practice meditation. The day you start, you will feel relaxed and calm because you will be relieving yourself from the crowd of thoughts that destroy your peace continuously.

Recent researches in cancer have found that cancer is caused when a person is in a state of depression. When a person is depressed, a hormone called luteinizing is overproduced by the body. This causes the cells in the body to multiply unrestricted, causing cancerous growths. Therefore, now we understand that depression is not only a disease of the mind, but can also damage the body, sometimes permanently.

The mind and the body are interconnected. You hurt the body, you hurt the mind, and visa versa. Whereas physical exercise is recommended to keep the body healthy, meditation is recommended to keep the mind healthy. If you do both, then you will enjoy the benefits that come with excellent health such as sharpness of mind, great concentration power, freedom from pains and diseases, a controlled temper, and greater joy and happiness.

Chapter 3. How to Start and What You Need

Many beginners quit because they use the most difficult techniques of meditation and are too hard on themselves. When you begin meditation, start small. Do not try to meditate for long hours. Keep it short and keep your focus. Even if you can meditate for five minutes continuously, it will be a feat.

You will find that concentrating even for one minute is difficult when you want to meditate while sitting. Your thoughts will wander again and again. You need to remember then that it is natural and is expected because your mind is not trained as yet. It is wild. Concentrate as the trick you have to go back most of the time. Even five minutes of this exercise will make you mentally stronger and in control.

Essential Things You Need for Meditating

The essential things that you need to meditate properly are:

a.) A suitable place,

b.) Time, and

c.) Willingness

It is best if you can choose a single place for meditation and practice it on a particular time every day. We are made up of habits. If you use the same place and the same time for meditation, you will quickly be in the meditative state because your mind is trained for this task whenever you are in that place during that time. A relative example that will help you to understand the importance of time and place will be this:

If you drink coffee every day at around 5 o'clock in the evening, and you had much work to do on a particular day, and you forgot to have your coffee, your mind will remind you of it and you will suddenly feel an emptiness or get a craving for coffee. That is what habits do to the mind. They train the mind. So, for best results, choose a particular place and time for meditating.

a.) Place: You should find a place that is quiet and comfortable. Make sure that nobody disturbs you while you're meditating. Any noises will easily distract you and will not allow you to be in the meditative state. If you think that a particular place will be quiet in the evening, then you may practice in the evening.

Having a quiet place for meditation is most essential because in the beginning you will find it easier to restrict your senses if you have no stimulants around. After you have practiced for many months, then you will be able to concentrate even when you can hear people talking or if there are noises around you. But in the beginning, choose a place where you cannot hear distracting sounds and where nobody can come to disturb you during the time you meditate.

To help yourself to concentrate, you may put on calming sounds that will assist you to meditate. This will also keep away the distracting noises that may make it hard for you to keep up your concentration.

b.) Time: As for the time, you can adjust the time according to your convenience. It gives best results if you can meditate in the morning. That will help you to have a stress-free day because the effect of meditation will stay with you throughout the day.

You can break down your meditation routine and practice once in the morning and once at night. If you can devote 30 minutes in a day, then you may practice for 20 minutes in the morning and 10 minutes before going to sleep. This will give you the most benefits because throughout your sleep you will be in a calm and peaceful state. You will find that you are sleeping better and are much more energetic and positive when you wake up in the morning.

c.) Willingness: If you are eager to meditate and are interested to be in the meditative state, then you will achieve it quickly. If you are skeptical, you must read as much literature as you can on it so that you can judge its importance. Before believing in it, try it with an open mind and see if it works for you.

Chapter 4. Meditation Techniques

There are various techniques that you can use to meditate. In the beginning, you can choose from a variety of techniques that are suitable for beginners. These techniques are relatively easier to follow than the more advanced ones. You may try any one technique and see how it works for you. Depending upon your power of concentration, your willingness, and the time you spend on meditation, any of the following techniques can be the right one for you.

Meditation Posture

When you sit down to meditate, choose a comfortable posture. Make sure that your back is straight and you can be totally at ease in that position for a long time. You may meditate sitting in the lotus position or lying straight on your back. You should not be conscious of your body when you are meditating. So, avoid moving as much as you can.

1. Sound Meditation

One of the best meditation techniques for beginners is sound meditation. In it, you listen to a sound that helps meditation and keep your concentration on that one sound. For the sake of simplicity, let us see how to do it step by step.

Step 1: Sit down in the lotus position or lie down flat on your back. Make sure that you are totally comfortable.

Step 2: Play the sound at a volume that is neither two high nor too low. It is best if the sound can bury other distracting sounds that may crop up. You can use the om chanting sound, sound of raindrops, sound of splashing water, instrumental music, or any other meditative sound that makes you feel calm and relaxed. You can find various kinds of meditation chants and sounds online.

Before you sit in meditation, ensure that whichever sound you are playing can play uninterrupted throughout the time period that you have chosen for meditating. When you are in a calm state of being is to be forced to get out of that state because the player stopped playing the music, this is the last thing you want to do.

Step 3: When the music begins, close your eyes and give your entire attention to that sound. Your mind will wander after a few seconds and you will begin to think different thoughts. This will happen unconsciously, so as soon as you become aware that you are thinking and not focusing on the sound, take back your full attention to that sound.

This cycle will repeat itself, but in time, you will find that your mind is wandering lesser and lesser, and you are able to concentrate on one sound for a long time.

Step 4: After you are done, you will feel very relaxed and peaceful. The impact of meditation on you will be instant. The duration of its impact will keep on increasing every day as you keep practicing.

2. Mindfulness Meditation

This technique of meditation involves concentrating on your breadth. When you are completely still, the only thing that you are conscious on being active is your breath. This is a very effective technique of meditation for beginners that do not require anything except a quiet place. Let us see how we can practice mindfulness meditation:

Step 1: Sit down in the lotus position or lie down straight on your back. Make sure that there are no sounds that you can hear.

Step 2: Begin to concentrate on your breath going in and out. Hear it and feel it. Try not to think but only to feel. Experience it.

As with any other technique of meditation, in the beginning you will be distracted and your mind will wonder. As so as you become aware that you have lost your concentration, bring it back to your breath.

Step 3: You may practice mindfulness meditation for 10-15 minutes every day. It is important to be consistent rather than to do a one-hour session once in three days. It is better if you can follow at 10 to 15 minute session every day, once or twice a day.

3. Body Scan

Similar to mindfulness meditation, in body scan instead of focusing your full attention on your breath, you place your complete attention on your body.

Start from your toes and slowly move up do your heels, calves, knees, thighs, groin, stomach and way up till your head. Repeat the process and you will slowly grow to heightened awareness. You will feel totally relaxed in your body and mind.

4. Meditation through thoughtlessness

This meditation technique is tougher than the others, but you may practice it just to see how it works for you. Different people have different capacities and preferences. It might be that one, even if harder, can suit you more than the easier ones even when you have just started to practice meditation.

As its name suggests, in this technique, you clear your mind of all thoughts. If you are able to do that even for a few seconds, it will be an achievement. There will be no experience that you have had like the one you will have when your mind if completely free from thoughts. To practice meditation through thoughtlessness, follow these steps:

Step 1: Sit in a lotus position or lie down on your back. Make sure that your back is straight and that you are comfortable.

Step 2: Close your eyes and be conscious of the thoughts in your mind. Remove the thoughts by removing your attention from them. You can transfer your attention to your breath to remove the thoughts. That will make it easy for you to remove thoughts. The thoughts will keep coming, but if you keep turning your conscious attention from them, they will not stay.

Step 3: To begin, practice only for five minutes or less at a time. Your mind is not as yet trained and will get tired after a while. Therefore, it is better to have short and intensive sessions.

Even if you are using another technique, you can practice meditation through thoughtlessness twice in a week. This is deep meditation and will heal you of painful memories, hurt, stress, anxiety, and depression. Through this meditation, you will be able to control your thoughts. If somebody said something bad to you and that thought is revolving in your mind continuously even then you want to forget about it, you can disallow that thought from entering your mind if you have thought control. All of negativity that are damaging your mental and physical health will help you free yourself.

5. Transcendental Meditation: Chanting of Mantra

Many people use the chanting of mantras to meditate. This is simpler method of meditating. In it, you mumble or chant aloud a set of words in repetition. Depending upon your language, religion or preference, you can use a chant that you believe in. You can even chant a single word. As a sound is coming out of your mouth, and you need to concentrate on that, it becomes easier to focus your attention.

Step 1: Close your eyes and begin the chanting. Make sure that you choose a pace and volume that you are comfortable with. You should determine the time period for the chanting so that you can be more focused.

Step 2: Place your complete attention on the sounds coming out of your mouth. Be aware of it. Keep your mind focused on the sounds for as long as you can.

Step 3: Take a break from the chanting when you feel tired or begin to chant in your mind. As long as you are focusing on the chant, you are meditating. It does not necessarily need to come out in the form of a sound.

This technique will reduce the myriad of thoughts crowding your mind. It will relax you and help you to develop your focus. To practice this technique, all you need is yourself and a quiet place.

6. Physical and Mental Relaxation Technique

To get the benefit of physical wellness as well as mental calmness, you can mix physical and mental relaxation. For beginners, this technique is highly recommended.

Step 1: Take a deep breath. Follow it with your mind. Keep your complete attention to the breath going into your lungs.

Step 2: Do not hold your breath. Breathe out slowly. Again, follow the breath going out with your mind.

Step 3: Repeat the process.

You may choose to do 5-10 deep breaths at a time. Remember that your mind will get tired of focusing after 3-5 breaths because it is not habitual to it. Therefore, it is best to keep the sessions short.

Step 4: Take a break of one minute. Thoughts should be in your mind, so just allow it to go thru your mind. Let your mind wander.

Step 5: Again, begin to deep breath and follow it with your complete focus.

This technique will give you the twin benefits of getting in more oxygen into your body, which will replenish your mind and body, and also relax your mind and improve concentration.

7. Buddhist Meditation: With Beads

The ultimate aim of meditation is to free the mind from thoughts. The techniques can be different, but the goal is the same. There are various kinds of techniques to meditate in Buddhist tradition. Here, we will look at meditation with beads because the other techniques are similar to the ones that we have discussed above.

Take a necklace or mala of beads. The beads should be big enough so that you can hold them between your fingers.

Step 1: Sit down in a lotus position.

Step 2: Hold the mala in your left hand.

Step 3: Hold a bead between your thumb and forefinger and say 'one'. You can say it aloud or in your mind.

Step 4: Move to the next bead and say 'two'. Carry on revolving the beads in your hand.

Step 5: Carry on counting. Instead of counting till a 100, it is better to count form 1 to 10 and then begin counting back from one.

Do it for 7-10 minutes without stopping. After you have become habitual to turning the mala in your hand, you can chant a mantra instead of counting. However, for beginners, counting is preferred because they can then focus on moving the beads between their fingers.

As with all the other techniques of meditation, this technique will make you feel relaxed and calm. It will align you to your inner self, your true self. You can carry your mala anywhere and begin to meditate. Even a five minute Buddhist meditation with beads will de-stress you completely.

Achieve Great Happiness and Joy

Instead of finding happiness in transient objects, find peace and happiness that stays forever inside you. You only have to unlock it. Meditation only promises what it can deliver. It is a tool to unlock the great potential that our mind has. You can achieve great happiness and joy by allowing yourself to be aligned with your true inner self. To realize it, you will, for a few minutes, let go of the attractions of the senses and allow yourself to be in the state of great calmness and peace where happiness lies. Once you begin to experience its benefits, it will become an important part of your life.

You can heal yourself from all pains, even if it's physical or emotional and even if it's psychological, through meditation. It acts on all levels: mental, physical, psychological and spiritual. Whether you are religious or not, you can practice meditation because it is an exercise of the mind and is not connected to any religion. It has the power to change your life for the best. As most of the best things in the world come for free, meditation too has no charges.

Conclusion

Meditation is not difficult to practice and it benefits you tremendously. It strengthens your focus, relaxes you, gives you good health, provides you with positivity and energy, and keeps you emotionally strong. Millions of people all around the world today are practicing meditation. It does not require you to spend money or buy any external equipment. You can easily enjoy great health just by training your mind to be in the best possible state that it can be in: the meditative state. Whether you are young or old, man or woman, religious or atheist, black or white, you can practice meditation and find yourself feeling more attuned to the higher consciousness.

Try meditating for 10 minutes today and see how you feel for the next one hour. Even a 10-minute meditation will relax you completely and make you feel more positive and energetic throughout the day. It is an exercise that will make you smarter, healthier and more at peace. Do not suffer from negativity, bad people and harsh circumstances; heal yourself from all pains by giving time to yourself. This will be the best few minutes that you will spend in your entire day.

Begin your new journey towards greater health and happiness today.

Thank You Page

I want to personally thank you for reading my book. I hope you found information in this book useful and I would be very grateful if you could leave your honest review about this book. I certainly want to thank you in advance for doing this.

If you have the time, you can check my other books too.

Lightning Source UK Ltd.
Milton Keynes UK
UKOW06f1056281215

265362UK00012B/226/P